The White House

by Mary Firestone
illustrated by Matthew Skeens

PICTURE WINDOW BOOKS
Minneapolis, Minnesota

Special thanks to our advisers for their expertise:

Kevin Byrne, Ph.D., Professor of History
Gustavus Adolphus College

Susan Kesselring, M.A., Literacy Educator
Rosemount–Apple Valley–Eagan (Minnesota) School District

Editor: Jill Kalz
Designer: Nathan Gassman
Page Production: Tracy Kaehler and Ellen Schofield
Creative Director: Keith Griffin
Editorial Director: Carol Jones
The illustrations in this book were created digitally.
Photo credit: Digital Stock, 22

Picture Window Books
1710 Roe Crest Dr.
North Mankato, MN 56003
www.capstonepub.com

Library of Congress Cataloging-in-Publication Data
Firestone, Mary.
The White House / by Mary Firestone ; illustrated by Matthew Skeens.
p. cm. — (American symbols)
Includes bibliographical references and index.
ISBN-13: 978-1-4048-2217-7 (library binding)
ISBN-13: 978-1-4048-2223-8 (paperback)
1. White House (Washington, D.C.)—Juvenile literature. 2. Washington (D.C.)—Buildings,
structures, etc.—Juvenile literature. 3. Presidents—United States—Juvenile literature. I. Skeens,
Matthew. II. Title. III. American symbols (Picture Window Books)
F204.W5 F53 2007
975.3—dc22   2006003378

Printed in the United States of America in North Mankato, Minnesota.
032014   008042R

Table of Contents

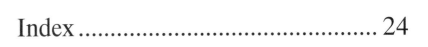

My name is Keneesha.
I'm a White House Secret Service agent. I'm here to show
you the most famous house in the country—the home and
office of the president of the United States.

4

The White House welcomes about 1,000 visitors every day!

The White House

The White House is an important symbol of leadership and democracy. It is where some of the most important decisions about the United States are made.

A New Home in a New City

George Washington picked the place for the White House in 1790. He chose a wooded area near the Potomac River.

The White House was part of a large project: to build a city for the U.S. government. That city became known as Washington, D.C.

Who Designed It?

The president's house had to be special. A contest was held to see who had the best design.

An Irishman named James Hoban won. His building looked a lot like Leinster House, a government building in Dublin, Ireland.

The first name for the White House was the President's House. It was later named the Executive Mansion. In 1901, President Theodore Roosevelt officially changed its name to the White House.

The First Family Moves In

The first president to live in the White House was John Adams, the second president of the United States. He moved in with his family in 1800, but the White House wasn't finished yet. There were no water pipes. The rooms had no heat. There was no place to dry the family's laundry. President Adams' wife, Abigail, had to hang clothes on ropes in the East Room!

The first president of the United States, George Washington, never lived in the White House. He was the only president who didn't live there.

Wartime and the White House

President James Madison and his wife, Dolley, moved into the White House in 1809. Sadly, during the War of 1812, the British burned the building. Only the outside walls survived the fire. After the war ended, the U.S. government rebuilt the White House on the site of the ruins. In 1817, the new president, James Monroe, moved in.

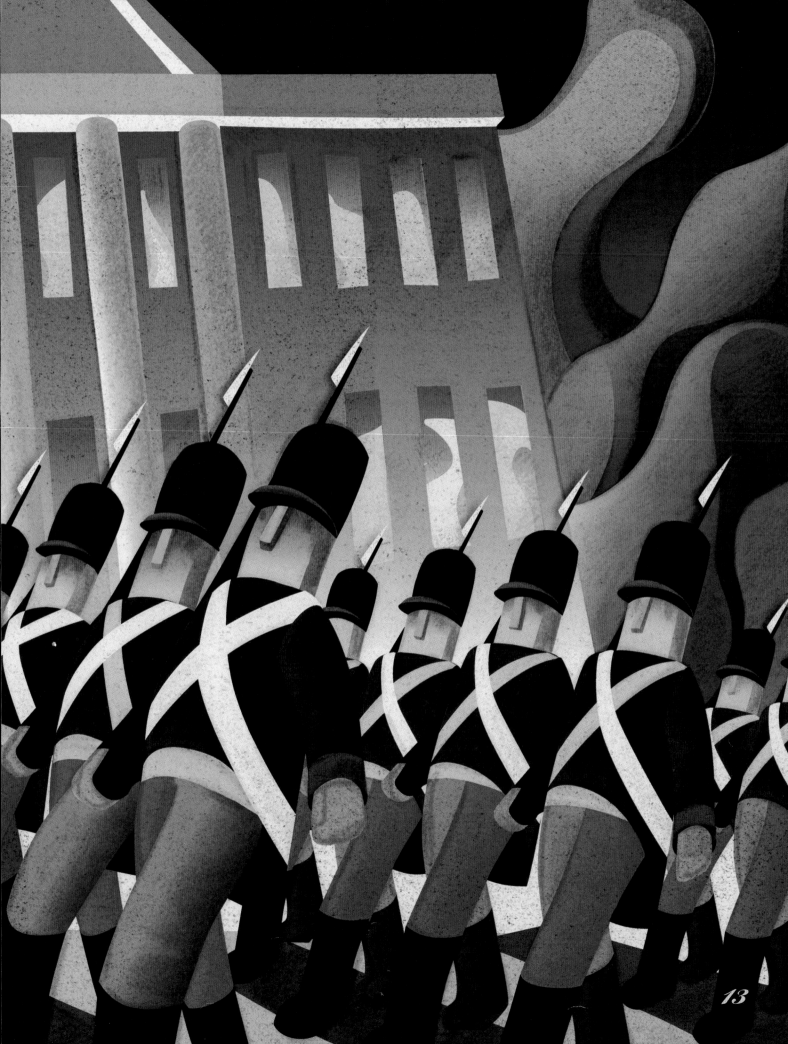

Growing Pains

Over the years, the White House changed many times, and in many different ways. The United States was growing, and so was the president's staff.

White House workers needed more space. More rooms, floors, the East Wing, and the West Wing were added to the building.

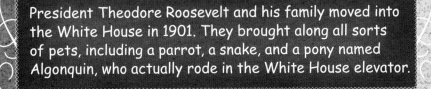

President Theodore Roosevelt and his family moved into the White House in 1901. They brought along all sorts of pets, including a parrot, a snake, and a pony named Algonquin, who actually rode in the White House elevator.

The Oval Office

The Oval Office is the president's office. The egg-shaped room was finished in 1909, when William Howard Taft was president. Every president since then has redecorated the office to suit his or her tastes. The Oval Office is in the West Wing, along with the Cabinet Room and the Situation Room. The West Wing is not open to visitors.

The original Oval Office was destroyed by fire in 1929. Workers built a new Oval Office in 1934 for President Franklin Delano Roosevelt. His office is the one used by today's president.

The Second Floor

The president and his or her family live on the second floor of the White House. This is also where the president's guests sleep when they spend the night. Overnight guests may sleep in the Rose Room or the Lincoln Bedroom.

President Abraham Lincoln never used the Lincoln Bedroom as a bedroom. When he was president, the room was his office. The room didn't become a bedroom until 1902, 37 years after Lincoln's death.

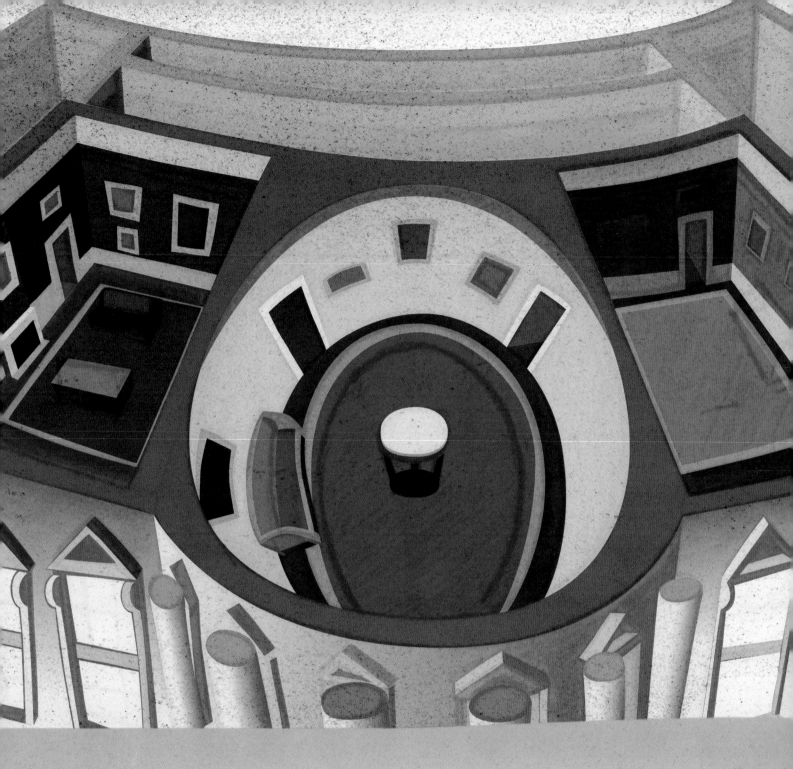

Colored Rooms

The White House is full of color! The Red Room, the Blue Room, and the Green Room are rooms where the president meets foreign leaders and other important guests.

The Ground Floor Corridor

Corridors are hallways. They lead from one part of the White House to another. From the Ground Floor Corridor, visitors can peek into the oval-shaped Diplomatic Reception Room. This is where the president welcomes ambassadors, kings, and queens.

The State Dining Room

The president and the first lady or first gentleman have dinner parties in the State Dining Room. As many as 140 guests can eat here at the same time.

I hope you enjoyed learning about the White House. If you'd like to come see us, call or write a congressman or congresswoman from your state. He or she may be able to send you tickets for a White House tour!

White House Facts

⚝ The original White House took eight years to build and cost about $230,000.

⚝ The White House is made of white-painted sandstone.

⚝ It takes 570 gallons (2,166 liters) of paint to cover the outside walls.

⚝ Did you know that the White House is much bigger than it looks? A lot of it is below ground or hidden by trees. It has:

- 6 stories
- 412 doors
- 147 windows
- 28 fireplaces
- 8 staircases
- 132 rooms and 35 bathrooms

- a tennis court
- a bowling lane
- a movie theater
- a jogging track
- a swimming pool

Glossary

ambassadors — the highest ranking people chosen to represent their country while visiting another country

Cabinet Room — the room where the president meets with the Cabinet, the leaders of the different departments (such as agriculture or finance) in the U.S. government

democracy — a kind of government in which the people make decisions by voting

Secret Service agent — a person whose main job is to protect the president

Situation Room — the room where the president meets with members of his or her staff to talk about urgent matters

staff — a group of people who work together for a common goal

symbol — an object that stands for something else

War of 1812 — (1812–1815) a war between the United States and Great Britain over unfair British control of shipping; often called the "Second War of Independence"

To Learn More

At the Library

Ashley, Susan. *The White House.*
Milwaukee: Weekly Reader Early
Learning, 2004.

Braithwaite, Jill. *The White House.*
Minneapolis: Lerner, 2004.

Grace, Catherine O'Neill. *The White
House.* New York: Scholastic, 2003.

O'Connor, Jane. *If the Walls Could
Talk.* New York: Simon & Schuster
Books for Young Readers, 2004.

On the Web

FactHound offers a safe, fun way to
find Web sites related to this book. All
of the sites on FactHound have been
researched by our staff.

1. Visit *www.facthound.com*
2. Type in this special code:
   1404822178
3. Click on the FETCH IT button.

Your trusty FactHound will fetch the
best sites for you!

Index

Look for all of the books in the American Symbols series:

The Great Seal of the United States
1-4048-2214-3
Our American Flag
1-4048-2212-7
Our National Anthem
1-4048-2215-1
The Statue of Liberty
1-4048-2216-X
The U.S. Constitution
1-4048-2643-2
The White House
1-4048-2217-8